D0111441

BLACK WITHIN
and
RED WITHOUT

Compiled by the Author

YOURS TILL NIAGARA FALLS

BLACK WITHIN AND RED WITHOUT

A DILLAR, A DOLLAR

TOUCH BLUE

BLACK WITHIN AND RED WITHOUT

A BOOK OF RIDDLES

COMPILED BY
LILLIAN MORRISON

ILLUSTRATED BY
Jo Spier

THOMAS Y. CROWELL COMPANY · NEW YORK

WITHDRAWN
CHILD LITERATURE COLLECTION
DELTA COLLEGE LIBRARY

For my nephew Robert
for Peter and Tommy
Eleonora
and Abdullah, Khadijah, Rizkah, and Dorria

Copyright 1953 by Lillian Morrison
All rights reserved. No part of this book may be
reproduced in any form, except by a reviewer,
without the permission of the publisher.
LIBRARY OF CONGRESS CATALOG CARD NO. 53-8420
Manufactured in the United States of America
Fifth Printing

CONTENTS

PREFACE

Riddles make you think and they make you laugh, but these, I hope, will provide something more than the fun in the game of guessing. They *sound* good. They had to have some feeling of myth or mystery, or some catchy quality of rhyme or rhythm to be included here. This is a collection of almost 200 traditional riddles, most of them in rhyme, and most of them still current orally in some part of the English-speaking world. (Just one is a translation from a foreign language—the "stone, grass, water" riddle on page 55). There are some "pun riddles" but the most common are those in which the answers are hidden in metaphors, some strongly imaginative or strangely evocative, others making up in sound or vitality what they lack in sense. Many of the rhymes are not only old nursery jingles but are also echoes of primitive chants, down-home folk ballads, lovely Elizabethan lyrics. And the strangeness of the world, the wonder and surprise at one's first discovery of the objects in it also come through them to us. In short, we have here much real poetry, of a playful, fresh, nonliterary kind to which people naturally respond.

Some of the riddles are extremely old. The beautiful snow riddle on page 30 has been found in a Latin translation in a manuscript of the tenth century. The riddle for man, known as the riddle of the Sphinx, is mentioned in the writings of the ancient Greeks. The year riddle on page 108, which compares the year to a tree, has been found in English in a fifteenth-century manuscript but is believed to date from ancient times. It has parallels in many parts of the world and Archer Taylor (see bibliography) believes it may be related to Oriental myths concerning the tree of life. A variation of the thorn riddle was known in Homer's day and the story goes that the poet's inability to solve it caused him to die of mortification.

Riddling in rhyme, once an adult pastime, is no longer so, except perhaps in isolated rural communities. Again, as with other forms of folklore, it is children, sensitive to the music in words and to the game in anything, who are preserving an old custom.

The sources of the riddles in this book are shown in the bibliography at the end.

Lillian Morrison

BLACK
WITHIN
AND
RED
WITHOUT

Guess a riddle now you must.
Stone is fire, and fire is dust.
Black is red, and red is white.
Come and view the wondrous sight.

Coal

Lily-low, lily-low, set up on end.
See little baby go out at town end.

A candle

Round as an apple
And thin as a knife.
Answer this riddle
And I'll be your wife.

A dime

What won't go up the chimney up,
  But will go up the chimney down?
What won't go down the chimney up,
  But will go down the chimney down?

An umbrella

3

Round and deep
And good to keep
Because you use it
Once a week.

The bathtub

Ten men's length,
Ten men's strength,
Ten men can't tear it,
Yet a little boy walks off with it.

A rope

Brass toes
Brass nose.
Upon my soul
It scares the crows.

A steam engine

4

Long waist,
Brazen face,
No thing of great beauty,
It stands most bright
By day and night
Performing of its duty.

A grandfather clock

Without a bridle
Or a saddle,
Across a thing,
I ride astraddle.
And those I ride,
By help of me,
Tho' almost blind,
Are made to see.

A pair of spectacles

Up and down, up and down,
Touching neither sky nor ground.

A pump handle

Black and white and read all over,
Goes from Halifax to Dover.

A newspaper

Round as an apple,
Flat as a chip,
Got two eyes,
And can't see a bit.

A button

Runs all day
But never runs away.

A clock

Opens like a barn door,
Wings like a bat,
Spread out your arms,
And jump in that.

A man's vest

What shoemaker makes shoes without leather,
With all the four elements put together?
Fire and water, earth and air;
Every customer has two pair.

A horse-shoer

9

Through the woods, through the woods I ran,
And as little as I am, I killed a man.

A bullet

Round as a riddle,
Deep as a spring.
Been the death of many
A pretty little thing.

A gun barrel

No mouth, no eyes,
Nor yet a nose,
Two arms, two feet,
And as it goes,
The feet don't touch the ground,
But all the way
The head runs round.

A wheelbarrow

Beyond the sea there is an oak,
And in that oak there is a nest,
And in that nest there is an egg,
And in that egg there is a yolk
Which calls together Christian folk.

A clapper in a bell in a steeple

I've seen you where you never were,
And where you never will be;
And yet within that very place,
You can be seen by me.

A mirror

What goes down the street,
Comes back home,
Sits in the corner,
And waits for a bone?

A shoe

Three little ladies, all dressed in white,
No use in the morning, but all in use at
night.

Candles

O'er the gravel I do travel,
   On the oak I do stand.
I ride a mare that never was foaled
And hold the bridle in my hand.

A sailor on board ship

13

Four legs up
And four legs down,
Soft in the middle
And hard all around.

A bed

Two big biscuits, one cup of coffee
Going to Augusta black and dirty.

A locomotive

Round as a biscuit,
Deep as a well.
Got as many windows
As a hotel.

A thimble

Riddlecum, riddlecum ruckup
What fell down and stuck up?

A fork

My face is marked,
My hands a-movin'
No time to play,
Got to run all day!

A clock

Sometimes with a head,
Sometimes with no head at all.
Sometimes with a tail,
Sometimes with no tail at all.
What am I?

A wig

As round as a pear
And as deep as a pail
If you want me to talk
You must pull my tail.

A bell

17

Niddy, noddy,
Two heads and one body.

A barrel

Brick upon brick,
Hole in the middle.
Guess that riddle,
I'll give you a fiddle.

A chimney

On the hill there is a house,
In that house there is a closet;
In that closet hangs a coat,
In that coat is a pocket, and
In that pocket is President Lincoln.

A penny

Round as a butter bowl,
Deep as a cup.
The Mississippi River
Cannot fill it up.

A strainer

As I looked out of my chamber window,
I heard something fall;
I sent my maid to pick it up
But she couldn't pick it all.

Powder

In open fields I cannot lie.
Within a box of ivory
My lady rest me quietly.

A fan of feathers

Little Nancy Etticoat
In a white petticoat
And a red nose;
The longer she stands,
The shorter she grows.

A lighted candle

As round as the moon,
As clear as crystal.
If you don't tell me that,
I'll shoot you with a pistol.

A watch

East, West, North, South,
A thousand teeth and no mouth.

A saw

As I went over yonder stile,
I met a thing that carried me a mile;
The cow calved it, the goose laid it,
It grew in a wood and the smith made it.

*A saddle, made of leather,
feathers, wood, and stones*

Mother, father, sister, brother,
All running after one another,
And can't catch one another.

The four wheels of a wagon

Two eyes I have which shine most bright,
Yet have I neither legs nor feet,
I have a mouth wherewith I bite,
But though I have, I never eat.

Scissors

Old Mother Twitchett had but one eye,
And a long tail which she let fly;
And every time she went through a gap,
A bit of her tail she left in a trap.

A needle

As I was going to Worcester,
I met a man from Gloucester.
I asked him where he was going,
And he told me to Gloucester
to buy something that had neither
top nor bottom, but which would hold
flesh, blood, and bone.

A ring

Headed like a thimble,
Tailed like a rat.
You may guess to Doomsday,
But you couldn't guess that.

A pipe

Flour of England, fruit of Spain,
Met together in a shower of rain,
Put in a bag, tied round with a string,
If you tell me this riddle, I'll give
you a ring.

A plum pudding

Brass button,
Blue coat,
Can't catch a billy goat.

A policeman

Wooden belly, iron back,
Fire in the hole, goes off with a crack.

A rifle

There was a man made a thing
And he that made it did it bring
But he 'twas made for did not know
Whether 'twas a thing or no.

A coffin

Crooked as a rainbow,
Teeth like a cat.
I bet a gold fiddle
You can't guess that.

A saw

I walk all day through rain and snow;
I scuff through sleet and hail;
I sleep a-standing on my head,
And my name it rhymes with *snail*.

A nail

Ten teeth without a tongue,
Good sport for old and young.
Take it out of its yellow fleece
And tickle it on the belly piece.

A fiddle

As I walked over a certain bridge,
I saw a rolling trout.
The more she eats, the more she drinks,
The more she spits it out.

A mill saw

As I was going over a bridge
I saw something in the hedge.
It had four fingers and one thumb
And was neither fish, flesh, fowl, nor bone.

A glove

What is long and slim, works in the light,
Has but one eye, and an awful bite?

A needle

Black within,
Red without.
Four corners
Roundabout.

A chimney

HIGHER THAN
THE STEEPLE

White bird featherless
Flew out from Paradise,
Perched upon yon castle wall.
Up came Lord Landless,
Took it up handless,
And rode away horseless
To the king's white hall.

Snow and sun

I've a tail like a flame.
Pray tell me my name.

A comet

What flies forever
And rests never?

The wind

Houseful, holeful
You can't catch a bowlful.

Smoke

I washed my hands in water
That never rained nor run;
I dried them with a towel
That was never wove nor spun.

Dew and sun

32

Arthur O'Bower has broken his band,
He comes roaring up the land!
The King of Scots with all his power,
Cannot turn Arthur of the Bower!

The north wind

Little hittle,
Wrapped in a whittle,
Nineteen times as high as St. Paul's Steeple.

A star

There was a thing just four weeks old
When Adam was no more.
Before that thing was five weeks old,
Old Adam was fourscore.

The moon

DELTA COLLEGE LIBRARY

I am no fish, no flesh, no voice.
But when I'm born, I make a noise.

Thunder

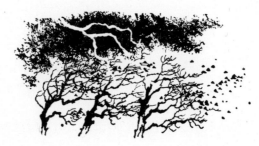

Through a rock, through a reel,
Through an old spinning wheel,
Through a hipper, through a clipper,
Through a basin full of pepper,
Through a horse's shin bone,
A riddle like this was never known.

Lightning

It's over the hills and hollows
And bites but never swallows.

Frost

The men of the East
Are plucking their geese
And sending their feathers
Here away, here away.

Snow

Who am I?
I come from the sky.
I wash the grass,
And over the road
You may hear me pass.

Rain

Lives in winter,
Dies in summer,
And grows with its root upward.

An icicle

I have a sheet and I can't fold it.
I have so much money I can't count it.
I have an apple and can't eat it.
I have a diamond and can't face it.

Sky, stars, moon, sun

In at every window
And every door crack,
Round and round the house
And never a track.

The wind

As red as an apple,
As round as a ball.
Higher than the steeple,
Weathercock and all.

The sun

37

In the last minute of my age
I do wax young again
And have so still continued
Since the world first began.

The moon

What is it that is higher than a house,
And yet it seems much lesser than a mouse?

A star in the sky

Hick-a-more, Hack-a-more,
Hung on a kitchen door.
Nothing so long and nothing so strong
As Hick-a-more, Hack-a-more
Hung on a kitchen door.

A sunbeam

I have a little sister, they call her
peep, peep;
She wades the waters deep, deep, deep;
She climbs the mountains high, high, high;
Poor little creature, she has but one eye.

A star

39

Goes to the door and doesn't knock,
Goes to the window and doesn't rap,
Goes to the fire and doesn't warm,
Goes upstairs and does no harm.

The sun

A milk-white gull through the air flies down,
And never a tree but he lights thereon.

Snow

Purple, yellow, red, and green,
The King cannot reach it, nor yet the Queen,
Nor can old Noll, whose power's so great,
Tell me this riddle while I count eight.

A rainbow

OUT OF THE
GROUND

Round as an apple,
Yellow as gold,
With more things in it
Than you're years old.

A pumpkin

A little house full of meat,
No door to go in and eat.

A nut

Daffy-down-dilly has come to town
In a yellow petticoat and a green gown.

A dandelion

Many eyes,
Never cries.

A potato

Old Mother Old,
She lives in the cold,
And every year she brings forth young,
And every one without a tongue.

An apple tree

Crooked as a ram's horn,
Flat as a plate,
Ten thousand horses
Can't pull it straight.

A river

Round as an apple,
Rough as a bear.
If you guess this riddle,
You may pull my hair.

A walnut

Ten thousand children beautiful
Of this my body bred;
Both sons and daughters finely decked;
I live, and they are dead.
My sons were put to extreme death
By such as loved them well;
My daughters died with extreme age,
But where I cannot tell.

Tree, fruit, and leaves

My father was a sprightly lad but now he's
dead and gone.
My mother was six hundred years old the minute I was born.
I was always brought up a suckling and never
eat no bread,
And never was good for nothing till after I was
dead.
They beat and banged me up and down and up
and down again,
Took my body from me, left nothing but my
skin.
Then I grew old and crazy near my constitu-
tion's end.
They took me all to pieces and blew me up
again.
I went among the poor and I went among the
rich.
At last they got sick of me and blew me all
to bits.

Flax

Round as a ball,
Sharp as an awl.
Those who can't guess
Are no account at all.

A chestnut burr

Way down on the hill there's a little green
house;
Inside that little green house is a little
white house;
Inside that little white house is a little red
house;
Inside that little red house are a whole lot
of little children.

A watermelon

Highty, tighty, paradighty, clothed all in
green,
The king could not read it, no more could
the queen.
They sent for a wise man out of the East,
Who said it had horns but was not a beast.

A holly tree

49

Runs all day and never walks,
Often murmurs, never talks.
It has a bed, but never sleeps.
It has a mouth, but never eats.

A river

What is it that stands uphill,
Stands downhill,
Stands still,
And goes to the mill?

A road

A patch upon patch
Without any stitches.
If you tell me this riddle,
I'll give you my breeches.

A cabbage patch

From house to house he goes,
A messenger small and slight,
And whether it rains or snows,
He sleeps outside all night.

A path

I went to the wood and caught it.
I sat me down and sought it.
Because I could not find it,
Home with me I brought it.

A thorn

As I was going through sloppery gap,
I met a little thing with a red cap,
A stone in its stomach, a stick in its side.
So answer me this, and I'll give you a ride.

A cherry

Cicely sage sits in her cage
And all her children die of age
Yet she is alive and lusty.

A tree and its leaves

As soft as silk,
As white as milk,
As bitter as gall,
A thick wall,
And a rough coat covers me all.

A walnut

As round as the moon
As yellow as ochre.
If you don't tell me that,
I'll fell you with the poker.

An orange

One says, "Let's go."
One says, "Let's stand."
One says, "Let's whisper."

A river, a stone, and grass

White as snow but snow it's not,
Green as grass but grass it's not,
Red as blood but blood it's not,
Black as ink but ink it's not.
What is it?

A blackberry

As I was going through my grandfather's lot,
I saw something that made me squat,
It looked so sweet and tasted so sour,
You can't guess that in half an hour.

A cranberry

FISH, FLESH, FEATHER AND BONE

Ears like a mule,
Runs like a fool,
Tail like a cotton ball.

A rabbit

A head like a snake, neck like a drake;
Side like a bream, back like a beam;
Tail like a rat, foot like a cat.

A greyhound

Long, slim, and slender,
Dark as homemade thunder,
Keen eyes and peaked nose,
Scares the devil wherever he goes.

A snake

Long leg and short thighs,
Rusty back and bullet eyes.

A frog

I'm a creature by travelers very
well known,
And walk on the ice in the north frigid
zone.

A bear

Jack-at-a-word ran over the moor,
Never behind but always before.

Will-o-the-wisp

It wasn't the moon,
It wasn't the stars,
But it lighted the fields.

Fireflies

He travels so much
And wherever he goes
He carries his trunk
At the end of his nose.

An elephant

As I went down that yellow bank,
I met a thing all rough and rank,
Two great lips and a hairy beard,
Darn the thing, it got me skeered.

A hog

There lives a prophet in the land
    His age no man can tell;
    His coat's of many colors,
    His boots are always new.
There is no tailor in the land
    Can shape to him or sew.

A rooster

I move without wings
Between silken strings.
I leave as you find
My substance behind.

A spider

Long man legless
Came to the door staffless
More afraid of a rooster and hen
Than he was of a dog and ten men.

A worm

Flip, flop, fleezy,
Slippery wet and greasy.
When it's out
It flops about,
Flip, flop, fleezy.

A fish

Little bird of paradise,
She works her work both neat and nice;
She pleases God, she pleases man,
She does the work that no man can.

A bee

As I went over Heeple Steeple
I met up with a heap o' people,
Some was nicky, some was nacky,
Some was the color of brown tobacky.

An anthill full of ants

As I was going across London Bridge,
I peeped down through a crack.
I saw old Mother Hubbard
With a blanket on her back.

A mud turtle

Runs and jumps,
Stops and humps.

A rabbit

Head like a cat, feet like a cat;
A tail like a cat, but it isn't a cat.

A kitten

Old Grandfather Diddle Daddle
Jumped in the mudpuddle,
Green cap and yellow shoes.
Guess all your loftiness
And you can't guess these news.

A frog

As I was going to Bramble Hall,
I heard an old man give a call.
His beard was meat, his mouth was horn;
Such a man was never born.

A rooster

Little Jessie Ruddle,
Sitting in a puddle,
Green garters and yellow toes;
Tell me this riddle or I'll punch your nose.

A duck in a puddle

A duck before two ducks,
A duck between two ducks,
A duck behind two ducks.

Three ducks

I'm called by the name of a man
   Yet I'm as little as a mouse;
When winter comes I'm often seen
With my red target near the house.

Robin redbreast

Behind the king's kitchen there is a great vat,
And a great many workmen working at that.
Yellow are their toes, yellow are their clothes.
Tell me this riddle and you can pull my nose.

Bees making honey

Down under the hill there was a mill;
In the mill there was a chest,
And in the chest there was a till;
In the till there was a cup,
And in the cup there was a drop.
No man could drink it,
No man could eat it,
No man could do without it.

The heart's blood

There was an apple on top of a tree.
Two men saw it,
Five picked it up,
Two heard it when it fell,
Ten put it up,
And one ate it.

Eyes, hand, ears, fingers, mouth

We never far asunder stray
Tho' we part a thousand times a day.

Eyelids

A little fence that's always wet,
But never has been rained on yet.

Teeth

A flock of white sheep
On a red hill.
Now they stamp, now they champ,
Now they stand still.

Teeth

I don't have it.
I don't want it.
But if I had it,
I wouldn't take the world for it.

A bald head

Two little holes in the side of a hill
Just as you come to the cherry-red mill.

Nostrils and mouth

As I looked over the castle wall
I saw a bunch of wands,
And nobody can count them
But God's own hands.

Hair of the head

What goes on four legs in the morning,
on two legs at noonday, and
on three legs at night?

Man, who crawls when he is a baby,
then walks on two legs,
and when old, walks with a cane

A HALF DOZEN
EGGS...

A lady in a boat
With a yellow petticoat.

An egg

Full to the brim
Without crack or seam.

An egg

A curtain drawn as fine as silk,
A marble stone as white as milk;
A thief appear and break them all,
Out start the golden ball.

An egg

Humpty Dumpty sat on a wall,
Humpty Dumpty had a great fall;
All the king's horses and all the king's men
Couldn't put Humpty-Dumpty together
again.

An egg

I had a little castle upon the seaside
One half was water, the other was land;
I opened my little castle door, and guess what
    I found;
I found a fair lady with a cup in her hand.
The cup was gold, filled with wine;
Drink, fair lady, and thou shalt be mine.

An egg

As I went through a field of wheat,
I picked up something good to eat.
Twas neither fish, nor flesh, nor bone
I kept it till it walked alone.

An egg

NOTHING SERIOUS

When first I appear I seem mysterious,
But when I'm explained I am nothing serious.

A riddle

Adam and Eve and Pinch-me-tight
Went over the river to see the fight.
Adam and Eve came back before night.
Now who was left to see the fight?

Pinch-me-tight
(Pinch the person
who gives the answer)

If hours were sold like hats and shoes,
What time of day would Adam choose?

Eve

A black sheep and a white sheep,
A horny sheep and one not;
A long-tailed sheep and a short-tailed sheep;
How many sheep have I got?

Two

I saw two boats
And only one man aboard.

A pair of shoes and one man

The moon nine days old,
The next sign to Cancer,
Pat rat without a tail,
And now, sir, for your answer.

Cleopatra

Riddledy, riddledy, riddledy rout,
What does a little boy hold in his hand
When he goes out?

The doorknob

'Tis in mountains, not in hills,
'Tis in meadows, not in fields,
'Tis in me and not in you,
'Tis in men and women too.

The letter m

There was a man, and no man
He had a gun, and no gun,
He shot a bird, and no bird,
Upon a tree, and no tree.

A boy with a popgun shot
a butterfly on a hollyhock

Two legs sat upon three legs,
With one leg in his lap;
In comes four legs,
And runs away with one leg.
Up jumps two legs,
Catches up three legs,
Throws it after four legs,
And makes him bring back one leg.

One leg—a leg of mutton
Two legs—a man
Three legs—a three-legged stool
Four legs—a dog

There was a man who had no eyes,
He went abroad to view the skies;
He saw a tree with apples on it,
He took no apples off, yet left no apples on it.

The man had one eye.
The tree had two apples on it.
He took one.

Three whole cakes, three half cakes,
Three quarters of another
Between the piper and his wife
And the fiddler and his mother.
Divide all that now if you can
But do not break the cakes, my man.

The piper's wife is the fiddler's mother,
so there are just three people
to divide the cakes among.

I know a word of letters three.
Add two and fewer there will be.

Few-er

As I was going to St. Ives,
I met a man with seven wives;
Each wife had seven sacks,
Each sack had seven cats,
Each cat had seven kits;
Kits, cats, sacks and wives,
How many went to St. Ives?

One, I myself

I see it.
You do not.
Yet it is nearer to you than to me.

The back of your head

They call me lace
The neck to grace
And yet I wot
That lace I'm not.

A necklace

It wasn't my sister nor my brother,
But still was the child of my father
and mother.
Who was it?

Myself

A word of three syllables seek till you find,
That has in it the twenty-six letters
combined.

Alphabet

A man looking at a portrait said:
Brothers and sisters
Have I none
But this man's father
Is my father's son.
What was the relationship between the
man looking and the man in the portrait?

Father and son

Come read me this riddle without any pother.
Five legs on one side and three on the other.
Two eyes in my forehead and four on my back.
One tongue that is silent and two that can
clack.

A horse carrying a woman and a man,
the woman riding side-saddle

Three legs up
Cold as stone.
Six legs down
Blood and bone.

*A man riding a horse with a
three-legged pot on his head*

What went to the North Pole and
stopped there,
And came back because it couldn't go
there?

A watch

Ten drag
Wooly bag
Over calf-hill.

Putting on a woolen stocking

A man at a river with a load of hay.
Bridge was away, ice was away.
How'd he get away?

The bridge was a way

A headless man had a letter to write.
It was read by one who had lost his sight.
The dumb repeated it word for word,
And he was deaf who listened and heard.

The letter o or "nothing"

Riddle, riddle me, Randy Row,
My father gave me some seeds to sow;
The seeds were black, the ground was white,
Riddle me that against Saturday night.

A boy writing in a book

THRICE I'VE
TOLD HER
NAME

There was a girl in our town
Silk an' satin was her gown,
Silk an' satin, gold an' velvet,
Guess her name, three times I've telled it.

Ann

What is that which belongs to you,
But others use it more than you do?

Your name

Elizabeth, Lizzy, Betsy, and Bess,
They all went together to seek a bird's
nest;
They found a nest with five eggs in it;
They each took one and left four in it.

Elizabeth, Lizzy, Betsy, and Bess
are all the same girl

Jim Damper rode across the bridge,
　　Bow, bow she bent to me,
Jim Damper rode across the bridge,
And Yet, he walked—how can it be?

Yet was the name of
Jim Damper's horse

There was a hill, you know,
And on the hill, you know,
There was a house, you know,
And in the house, you know,
There was a table, you know,
And under the table, you know,
There was a dog, you know.
What was his name, you know?

Uno (*You know*)

The king of Morocco built a ship,
An' in that ship his daughter sits,
An' I tell her name I am to blame,
An' there's three times I've told her name.

Ann

Down in the dark dungeon
There sits a brave knight,
All bridled, all saddled,
All ready to fight;
Call me his name for the brass of my bow,
I've told you three times now
And still you don't know!

The knight's name is All

As I went over London Bridge
There I met a man;
He tipped his hat, and drew his cane,
And in this riddle I told his name.

Andrew

103

There was a king met a king
In a narrow lane
Said the king to the king
Where have you been?
I have been a hunting
The buck and the doe.
Will you lend me your dog?
Yes, I will do so;
Call upon him, call upon him.
What is his name?
I have told you twice
And won't tell you again.

*The men's names were King
and the dog's name was Bin*

There is a school upon a hill,
And in the school there is a bell,
And what's the teacher's name?

Isabel

Seven big pears was hangin' high,
Seven big men come a-ridin' by
Each lit down and took him a pear.
How many pears was left a-hangin' there?

Five. One of the men was named Each
and he took a pair

An' it's neither Peg, Meg, nor Margit
Is my true love's name;
An' it's neither Peg, Meg, nor Margit,
An' thrice I've told her name.

Ann

THE BEGINNING OF EVERY END....

I have a tree of great honor,
Which tree beareth both fruit and flower;
Twelve branches this tree hath nake,
Fifty-two nests therein he make,
And every nest hath birds seven;
Thank-ed be the King of Heaven;
And every bird hath a different name:
How may all this together frame?

The tree is the year;
the twelve branches are the twelve months;
the fifty-two nests are the fifty-two weeks;
the seven birds are the seven days in the week
and each one has a different name.

What is that which no man ever yet did see,
Which never was, and always is to be?

Tomorrow

Read my riddle, I pray:
What God never sees,
What the king seldom sees,
What we see every day.

An equal

What do contented men desire,
The poor have and the rich require,
The miser spends, the spendthrift saves,
And all men carry to their graves?

Nothing

Something red
Under the pot
Makes it hot.

Fire

Light as a feather,
Nothing in it.
A stout man can't hold it
More than a minute.

A breath

There is a thing that nothing is,
 And yet it has a name.
It's sometimes tall and sometimes short,
 It joins our walk, it joins our sport
 And plays at every game.

A shadow

I tremble at each breath of air
And yet can heaviest burdens bear.

Water

As I went over London Bridge,
I peeped into a winder,
I saw four-and-twenty ladies
Dancing on a cinder.

Sparks

Riddle my riddle rocket,
You can't hit it
And I can't knock it.

Smoke

I have a little cow,
She sits in her stall.
Give her much, give her little,
She'll eat it up all.
Give her wind and she'll fly,
Give her water and she'll die.

Fire

Over the water,
Under the water,
Round the world it ranges.
Never been seen by the eye of man,
But oftentimes it changes.

The mind

The beginning of eternity,
The end of time and space,
The beginning of every end
And the end of every place.

The letter e

BIBLIOGRAPHY

Almost all the riddles in this book are from printed sources. A glance at the titles below will show the wide geographic distribution of the riddles—from our own Ozarks to Jamaica, West Indies and the British Isles. Before listing the various folklore journals, chapbooks, collections of nursery rhymes, and other printed materials from which they have been gathered, I would like to give special mention to that monumental work by Archer Taylor *English Riddles from Oral Tradition* (University of California Press, 1951). This comprehensive and scholarly book led me to many sources I might not otherwise have found. My thanks also to the many folklorists listed below who collected "in the field" and whose original source material has vitalized this collection.

Backus, E. M. "Notes and Queries." *Journal of American Folklore,* vol. 48, 1935.

Bacon, A. M. and E. C. Parsons. "Folklore from Elizabeth City County, Virginia." *Journal of American Folklore,* vol. 35, 1922.

Baring-Gould, S. "Yorkshire Household Riddles." *Notes and Queries,* 3rd series, vol. 8, 1865.

Beckwith, Martha. *Jamaica Anansi Stories.* Memoirs of the American Folklore Society, XXVII. New York, 1924.

Boggs, R. S. "North Carolina White Folktales and Riddles." *Journal of American Folklore,* vol. 47, 1934.

The Booke of Meery Riddles. London, 1629. Reprinted in J. O. Halliwell-Phillipps' *Literature of the 16th and 17th Century.* London, 1851.

Brewster, Paul G. "Riddles from Southern Indians." *Southern Folklore Quarterly,* vol. 3, 1939.

Burne, Charlotte Sophia. *The Handbook of Folklore.* London, 1914.

Chambers, Robert. *Popular rhymes, fireside stories and amusements of Scotland*. Edinburgh, 1842.

Chappell, J. W. "Riddle Me, Riddle Me, Ree," *Folk-Say*, vol. 2, 1930.

Compton's Pictured Encyclopedia and Fact Index, vol. 12. "Riddles." Chicago, 1952.

Cuthbertson, W. F., ed. *Rhyme a Riddle*. London, 1946.

Daiken, Leslie. *Children's Games Throughout the Year*. London, 1949.

Day, Mahlon. *New Riddle Book*, printed and sold by Mahlon Day. New York, 1829.

Emrich, Marion Vallat, and George Korson. *The Child's Book of Folklore*. New York, 1947.

Farr, T. J. "Riddles and Superstitions of Middle Tennessee," *Journal of American Folklore*, vol. 48, 1935.

Fauset, Arthur Huff. *Folklore from Nova Scotia*. Memoirs of the American Folklore Society, XXIV. New York, 1931.

Fitzgerald, David. "Of Riddles," *Gentleman's Magazine*, vol. 251, 1881.

Gardner, E. E. *Folklore from the Schoharie Hills*. Ann Arbor, 1937.

Greenleaf, Elizabeth B. "Riddles of Newfoundland," *The Marshall Review*, vol. 1, no. 3, 1938.

Greenway, Nellie. *Fifteen Hundred Riddles*. New York, 1904.

Guess Again; a choice collection of entertaining riddles arranged by Peter Puzzlewit, Esq. New York, 184?.

Halliwell-Phillipps, J. O. *The Nursery Rhymes of England*. New York, 1886.

————. *Popular Rhymes and Nursery Tales*. London, 1849.

Hubbard, Alice, and Adeline Babbitt. *The Golden Flute*. New York, 1932.

Hudson, Arthur Palmer. *Specimens of Mississippi Folklore*. Ann Arbor, 1928.

Hyatt, Harry Middleton. *Folklore from Adams County, Illinois*. Memoirs of the Anna Egan Hyatt Foundation. New York, 1935.

John-the-giant killer, esq., pseud. *Food for the mind*. London, 1778.

Landon, Melville D. *Wit and Humor of the Age*. Chicago, 188?.

Leather, Ella M. *The Folk-Lore of Herefordshire*. London, 1912.

McCall, P. J. "Folklore Riddles—Irish and Anglo Irish," *Journal of the National Literary Society of Ireland*, vol. 1, 1900.

MacGréine, Padraig, O. S. "A Longford Miscellany," *Bealoideas*, vol. 3, 1931-1932.

Neal, Janice. "Wa'n't That Remarkable!" *New York Folklore Quarterly*, vol. 1, 1945.

Opie, Iona, and Peter Opie. *The Oxford Dictionary of Nursery Rhymes*. London, 1952.

Parker, Angelina. "Oxfordshire Village Folk-Lore, II," *Folk-Lore*, vol. 34, 1923.

Parsons, Elsie Clews. "Folklore from Aiken, South Carolina," *Journal of American Folklore*, vol. 34, 1921.

―――. *Folklore of the Antilles, III*. Memoirs of the American Folklore Society, XXVI, Part 3. New York, 1943.

―――. "Bermuda Folklore," *Journal of American Folklore*, vol. 38, 1925.

―――. "Notes on the Folklore of Guilford County, North Carolina," *Journal of American Folklore*, vol. 30, 1917.

―――. *Folklore of the Sea Islands, South Carolina*. Memoirs of the American Folklore Society, XVI. New York, 1923.

―――. "Folklore of the Cherokee of Robeson County, North Carolina," *Journal of American Folklore*, vol. 32, 1919.

Perkins, A. E. "Riddles from Negro School Children in New Orleans." *Journal of American Folklore,* vol. 35, 1922.

Potter, Beatrix. *The Tale of Squirrel Nutkin.* New York, 1903.

Potter, Charles Francis. "Riddles." *Funk & Wagnalls Standard Dictionary of Folklore, Mythology and Legends,* vol. 2, 1950.

Praeger, S. Rosamond. "Riddles from County Down,"*Bealoideas,* vol. 4, 1933-34.

———. "Rimes and Riddles from County Down," *ibid,* vol. 8, 1938.

Randolph, Vance, and Isabel Spradley. "Ozark Mountain Riddles," *Journal of American Folklore,* vol. 47, 1934.

Redfield, W. A. "A Collection of Middle Tennessee Riddles," *Southern Folklore Quarterly,* vol. 1, 1937.

Rorie, David. "Some old Scottish Rhyming Riddles," *Scots Magazine,* vol. 23, no. 2, 1935.

Taylor, Archer. *English Riddles from Oral Tradition.* Berkeley, 1951.

Thurston, Helen S. "Riddles from Massachusetts," *Journal of American Folklore,* vol. 18, 1905.

The Trial of Wit; or a new riddle book. Printed by C. Randall. 1795.

Tupper, Frederic, Jr. "The Holme Riddles (M. S. Harl. 1960)," *Publications of the Modern Language Association,* XVIII, 1903.

Waugh, F. W. "Canadian Folklore from Ontario," *Journal of American Folklore,* vol. 31, 1918.

Wells, Carolyn. *All for Fun.* New York, 1933.

Wood, Ray. *The American Mother Goose.* New York, 1938.